Recycle It!

Paul Humphrey

Illustrated by
Jon Davis

TOMNACROSS
PRIMARY SCHOOL
Evans

Everything that is put
into the containers is
used again.

This is where the bottles come for recycling.

All the labels and tops are taken off the bottles at the glass recycling plant.

Then the bottles are broken into small pieces.

The broken glass is taken to a glass factory. It is melted in a giant furnace and used to make new bottles and jars.

So the bottle that I put into the bottle bank might be a jam jar by next week!

14

15

The old cans are separated. The steel cans go into one container and aluminium cans go into another. Can you see how that is done?

Oh yes, with a big magnet!

The steel cans
stick to the magnet
but the aluminium
ones don't.

17

Then the cans are sent to an aluminium mill or to a steel mill.

What is happening to the cans now?

18

The cans are being melted
down and made into new
metal things.

19

Old newspapers are sent to this paper mill. They are torn up and mixed with water.

Then they are made into new paper and cardboard.

I've got a pad of recycled paper at home.

21

The charities pass the old
clothes on to needy people.

Lots of things can be recycled. Some plastic bottles can be recycled and made into new plastic.

If we didn't recycle things we would need more rubbish dumps. That's bad for our environment. Dumps spoil the land.

Recycling saves money and it is good for the environment.

I'm going to recycle as much as possible.

Can you remember how each of these things is recycled? Look back at the book to help you.

Paper

Cans

Bottles